1 PIANO, 4 HANDS • INTERMEDIATE LEVEL

BILLY JOEL
FOR PIANO DUET

ISBN 978-1-4950-0912-9

HAL•LEONARD®
CORPORATION

7777 W. BLUEMOUND RD. P.O. BOX 13819 MILWAUKEE, WI 53213

In Australia Contact:
Hal Leonard Australia Pty. Ltd.
4 Lentara Court
Cheltenham, 3192 Victoria, Australia
Email: ausadmin@halleonard.com.au

Visit Hal Leonard Online at
www.halleonard.com

C O N T E N T S

IT'S STILL ROCK AND ROLL TO ME

Words and Music by
BILLY JOEL

JUST THE WAY YOU ARE

Words and Music by
BILLY JOEL

D.S. al Coda

D.S. al Coda

THE LONGEST TIME

Words and Music by
BILLY JOEL

CODA

MY LIFE

Words and Music by
BILLY JOEL

NEW YORK STATE OF MIND

Words and Music by
BILLY JOEL

SHE'S ALWAYS A WOMAN

Words and Music by
BILLY JOEL

PIANO MAN

Words and Music by
BILLY JOEL

UPTOWN GIRL

Words and Music by
BILLY JOEL